M000103344

Battles & Lullabies

Poems by

Richard Michelson

University of Illinois Press

Urbana & Chicago

For Bob + Judy —

[signature]

Battles
& Lullabies

© 2006 by Richard Michelson
All rights reserved
Manufactured in the United States of America
∞ This book is printed on acid-free paper.
1 2 3 4 5 C P 5 4 3 2 1

Library of Congress Cataloging-in-Publication Data
Michelson, Richard.
Battles and lullabies : poems / by Richard Michelson.
p.   cm. — (Illinois poetry series)
ISBN-13: 978-0-252-03061-1 (acid-free paper)
ISBN-10: 0-252-03061-3 (acid-free paper)
ISBN-13: 978-0-252-07303-8 (pbk. : acid-free paper)
ISBN-10: 0-252-07303-7 (pbk. : acid-free paper)
I. Title. II. Series.
PS3563.I34B38   2005
8113.54 — dc22   2005012419

For my wife, Jennifer, my mother, Caroline,
and in memory of my father, Maurice Michelson

When a man dies, they say "He was gathered unto his fathers."
As long as he is alive, his fathers are gathered within him . . .
—Yehuda Amichai

Contents

▮▮▮ ⋀⋁ Bathing by Candlelight

▮▮▮ ⋁ The Jews that We Are

Battles & Lullabies

Counting to
Six Million

Gift-Wrapping the Garbage

My father's gift-wrapping the garbage.
"Bee—you—tee—full," he says.
Four bundles, and his accent (Brooklyn)
wraps like a bow around each.

Eight days into the strike
and the world smells like soup.
"Kreplach soup," he says.
"Your Aunt Ida's.
Know what I mean?"

My son can't picture it—
the neighborhood,
its poverty—
and I've lost the point,
trying to explain myself.
"Poor," I'm yelling. "Poor."
And suddenly my eyes are popping
like Dangerfield's on Letterman,
until my son takes pity.
"OK," he asks, "how poor?"

"Laugh," my father says, "if you want to,
but don't they all love Christmas?"
His accent is on the *they,*
but weren't times different then?

It was a Jewish neighborhood
and then it was a Negro neighborhood
until the Puerto Ricans drove out the Blacks.
Shvartzers, I used to say
and *Schwartzes,* would echo back.

"Stop talking garbage,"
 my mother says, but
 aren't I my father's son?

"Every problem," he taught me
"has a solution,"
 and I've got to tell you, *they*
 stole that garbage
 lickety-split.

We danced together, clapping
 like two comics
 in a Catskill routine. Me, squealing
 with my *kvitchadicker* voice
 (high and squeaky),
 as I held onto him,
 held onto him,
 tight.

"How tight," my son asks,
 but just now I'm not in the mood
 for his sarcasm. I'd rather weep.
 I'd rather watch this old newsreel—
 my father working himself to death,
 I mean literally, and dying out on the street,
 lying there, maybe an hour,
 one   more   dead   Jew.

"Take out the damn garbage," I tell my son.
 Sure, I'd rather hug him, but right now
 isn't my heart on the roller coaster
 at Coney Island, and I'm barely holding on?

Like Nobody's Business

Business, my father says, *was never so good.*
He means it's never been good—it's never been good enough—
it's never been better. He's copying master keys,
installing iron gates. Even the cops spraying paint
to cover the graffiti, Edie says, on each other's asses.
Shakespeare, my father shouts, *should hear such language.*

I'm ten then, half my own son's age, and still in love
with the piercing scream of my own soprano.
Caruso, my father calls, *let's sell some garbage cans.*
And suddenly I'm in the cellar—flashlight jammed in my innocent mouth—
climbing past cement bags stacked like combat casualties,
my single beam blinding rats with each turn of my head.

This, I know, is like nobody's business:
I'm hammering 36 gallons of heavy-gauge galvanized steel against the wall,
pounding until its open mouth twists in pain and confusion,
its back bent over: my own apocryphal Jewish immigrant grandfather
guarding his brand new Naugahyde American wallet.
Picasso, my father calls me, *with a ball-peen.*

It's a war on poverty, I tell my son.
We're driving through the old neighborhood, and I'm boring even myself,
pointing out the burned-out empty lots, like they're holes in my own heart.
Maybe it's nothing but misplaced nostalgia, this detour on his last day home.
Maybe all I'm wanting is to remember my own father's face,
dumbfounded by a whole dorm of Darwins, a metropolis of Einsteins.

Work, he finally said, *like nobody's business, and never, ever look back.*
He'd never have believed that the farther ahead we stare,
the further we travel back into time. The astronomers are right, I tell my son,
your future's in this rearview mirror, sneaking up from behind.
We're turning past the tenements, idling on Pitkin
where I pre-smashed each shiny new trash can before it could be stolen.

Why throw myself down on this corner now?

Here, I want to say, they'd still kill a man for a quarter,
but I'm silent instead, counting down the quarter-century since I've been back.
I can still hear Edie wailing over the phone: *Your father, gunshot, heart attack.*
Antigone, he might have groaned, if he wasn't still busy bleeding,
not in his mind's battlefield, but in this real, random, ravaged, empty gutter,
hundreds of miles between us. All alone.

It's getting dark, my son says, removing his headphones.
Just this second he's decided to double major in business and philosophy.
He wants to think, he tells me, about making a lot of money.
I know I'm supposed to laugh, or at least let the rich baritone of his voice
lead us all the way back home. But even so I turn aside, because just now,
how I'm feeling, I know, is nobody's business but my own.

Life Insurance

How about that electricity! my wife's grandfather says.
He's bounding his eighty years down the stairs, one-handing his umbrella,
to help me uncurl my prematurely shtetl'd back
out of this once luxurious cotton pullover of a VW
that somehow downsized itself, compacting
throughout our aching eight-hour drive through the storm.

Ain't it something, he says, *the way, whoosh, it comes back on,
lighting up the whole county, all eighty houses burning like candles
on a vanilla village-sized birthday cake.*

I'm already disarmed; the unaffected wisdom, the unprejudiced enthusiasm.
He's never met, my wife says, a real Jew before,
and I, resisting the urge to ask about imposters, watch him walk seven times
around this Wedding Chuppah of a wagon, kicking each tire, questioning
my engine's horsepower, and counting out, I could tell, real horses.

I'm thinking as he moves about the wonder of the small engine that drives
     his body,
and I'm judging my own grandfathers—stirring their years together,
but even this new imaginary grandfather refuses to live
long enough for me to be born. It's not only a history of heart failure,
and colon cancer, but history itself,
the imperturbable iron horse, the houses burning down like candles.

Amazing! my wife's grandfather says. He's bent over the fan belt, testing its
     elasticity,
dismantling the automatic choke, while I, charmed and disoriented,
twirl imaginary side-locks before setting off like a dachshund at his heels.

All that was twenty years ago, and ever since
my lower lumbar's been arguing this entire two-day drive—
eight hours up and back the next, still no airport nearby—
each year his possible last, while our new Teutonic tank-sized SUV
conjured up one child, and then the next.

What if just once we don't go, I beg my wife, but she's already loading the
        valises,
looking now like one of those Biblical old-world water carriers, and now
a smooth-skinned milk maiden grown up on the fresh air of her
        grandfather's farm.

Maybe it is only centuries of suffering and Jewish guilt that keep the world alive,
I say, sounding as if my living depended on selling life insurance to
        centenarians.
I'm comfortable now, stretched out in the back, heels up on our luggage,
making guttural noises, imagining myself as a grandfather,
while up front my youngest swerves in the driver's seat, the roads clogged
with hundredth-birthday revelers, thirty-six great grandchildren
        converging
like electrons on the nucleus of a one-horse town.

My hope for my own children is not that they live forever,
but try explaining that to a teenager at the wheel of a car.
How much life insurance do you have? my son asked me once.
He was eight at the time, already counting out an inheritance,
calculating his share of the world. *Watch the road!* I yell,
angry for no reason after all these years, except that I'm growing tired
and suddenly scared. It's almost sundown and I still don't understand

how the electricity travels from one lamppost to the next, lighting up the
    future
as if it's daybreak on the horizon and we have all the time in the world.

Green Bananas

The way my grandmother put back the green bananas,
unwilling to make an investment in her future,
is how I'm feeling this evening, watching my grown children watching CNN,
sitting side by side on the sofa—no shoving, no teasing, no tattling—
just image upon image of Armageddon: starvation, explosion, long lines
at the gas pump, and even the Rabbi abandoning town.

Biological, I hear my son say. And my daughter answers: *no, chemical*
or, perhaps, *nuclear.* I'm too embarrassed just now to admit how happy I am
to have them home again, even for this single moment, even though
they insist they're only visitors, on vacation, no longer *at home.*

I built my house too close to the water, my grandmother used to say
whenever I left in a hurry, or stayed away too long.
She meant she was easily moved to tears, but it took my own mother years
to teach me the impossibility of protecting the weak from the strong.

Enough crying, she'd say, clicking her tongue like she was laying down dominoes,
contesting the intricate but historical patterns of sudden death.
She meant, I now know, to comfort me, to protect me from her brother's tank
turned unexpectedly upside down in Germany, the long lines at the gas pump,

the clergy, every denomination, blissfully but, pardon me, stupidly,
following their prayers back home. O but then she'd kiss whatever ailed me,
while my sister railed against all injustice, her theme song exploding
over the single cushion separating what she did right from all I'm still doing
    wrong.

How can we expect world peace, my father would have said,
—if he had been paying attention, if he wasn't at that very moment watching
I Love Lucy's long slide across the world's stage on an overripe banana—
when under one roof my own two children can't even get along.

As for me, just now I'm setting the table and filling the fruit bowl,
whistling like Ricky Ricardo, unaware of his wife's grand schemes,
the well-intentioned but certain and coming disaster. *Don't die yet, Grams,* I say
holding her tightly in the aisle, unashamed of my tears.
But of course, I tell my kids, she died anyhow, falling headfirst into the honeydews,
scattering melons like hand grenades every which way.

Undressing Aunt Frieda

Undressing Aunt Frieda, I think of how,
undressing me, she would tilt back her head
as if listening for footsteps, the faint marching
of the S.S. men whose one great dream
was her death. They must have feared
how her young Jewish fingers unbuttoned
and buttoned, as if they had continents
to cross, as if here, in East New York,
I was already tiring, and no one at home
to put me to bed.

Undressing Aunt Frieda, I try to imagine her
healthy, undressing herself, slowly at first,
as if for the love of a man, untying
her green-checkered apron with the secret pockets,
unwrapping the frail *just-shy-of-five-feet* body
whose scarred beauty Rubens would surely have missed,
but Rembrandt, in the loneliness of his dying days,
might have immortalized.

My daughter at my side grows restless.
She unties her shoes, tugs at each sock.
She has learned, recently, to undress herself,
and pausing occasionally for applause,
does so now. Naked, she shimmies up onto the bed,
curls her thin fingers around Frieda who,
as if she wished herself already dead,
doesn't coo or even smile.

A dream of love, Frieda preached, *is not love,*
but a dream. And bad luck, I'd say, *follows*
the bitter heart. But undressing her now,
I remember the lightness of her hands
and their strength, which somehow lifted me
above the nightmares she had known.
I'll care for you, she whispered once
as if you were my own. My daughter yawns.
I lift her gently, hoping she'll sleep
the hour drive home.

Undressing My Daughter

Gently, I lift her jersey up, inside out,
over the boiled peach of her stomach,
a color I recognize as my wife's, after love.
The sweater, knitted snug, hugs her neck,
as I, pulling awkwardly from above,
feel a young girl's instinctive fear
of darkness, arms trapped above her head.

I tug violently until she breaks,
triumphant, into the light, her face
distorted in the grimace of birth.
Would you love me, she asks,
curling her lower lip past sensuality
into an exaggerated pout,
if I looked like this? I hold her,

knowing tonight she will not sleep,
her eyes held open by the oxygen tanks
that keep her Great Aunt Frieda alive.
What, my wife whispers, *did you expect?*
To bring a child! And she,
unfastening her chemise,
now speaks of death with dignity.

Would you love me, she asks,
enough to let me die? And I,
once again, her breathless
half-dressed lover,
mistaking Aunt Frieda's footsteps
for the beat of my own heart,
know I am trapped.

Yes, I tell my daughter. *Yes!*
But she's already fast asleep
and only I remain awake,
listening to the silence
between her breaths;
the sound of Aunt Frieda
who cannot stop breathing.

Halloween

Her face, blood-streaked, is no longer my daughter's.
She'll wear no lace this year, no tiaras, no bows.
She bobs, fangs bared, through the thin skin of water.
She's bitten the apple. Triumphant, she goes
to collect her prizes. And I'm left to remember
my own father sewing, under my collar,
a blood-stained cape. His warning, like thunder,
still rings in my ears. With each stitch he'd holler
Beware the God-damned sons'a'bitches
with their poisons and candy bait. Now I wait
for my daughter, who has entered a night full of witches.
Gone, before I could kiss her goodnight.
And the doorbell keeps singing: *too late, too late.*
Even the full moon is missing a bite.

I Wish He Had Died Then, His Body

I wish he had died then, his body
under mine, less like a wrestler pinned
for the count than a lover before sleep
but after love. My mouth on his mouth
breathing in the short frantic bursts
I would not breathe again for six years
when, coaching my wife through labor,
I watched her push into this life the child
already named with his name. I wish
he had died then, although then I prayed

for his breath to answer mine, his arms
to lift me easily as I, saying her name,
lift my new daughter to her mother's breast
and turn to call my own mother who,
even in her joy, will remember
this hospital, its walls the soiled white
of the handball court where, proud
to see his son control the game,
but his own pride even stronger, my father dove,
forgetting his age, his family, his tired heart.

I wish he had died then, his body
hovering before it fell, the way the ball,
gently kissing the left front corner, hovered,
so quietly I could hear myself remembering how,
home late from work, or leaving early,
he would kiss the air above me
while I feigned sleep. I wish he had died then,
his body in my arms, instead of dying
alone in the street, my telephone ringing
like my daughter's first cry.

Counting to Six Million

I.

Sleep faster, my son says.
He's poking at my eyelids, pulling at the pillows,
the helicopter hum of anticipation rising in his throat
as I reach out and spin him onto the bed.

I want to set my heels once more in the soft underbelly of his childhood,
airlift him from danger, from disease, from all his fears,
which are maybe not even his fears at all, but only mine.
Yet now as he hovers above me, my body splayed out
like my father's before me, my every breath is less a prayer
than a love letter torn open in desperation.

II.

Remember, I say, when we counted to six million,
a visualization of tragedy, one half hour a day for two years,
and that, for the tribe only;
it would have been another whole year for the gypsies, the Catholics,
the gays, the foreigners, the Negroes, the artists, the philosophers, etc.

You were barely six at the time, your mother wondering
what the hell I was thinking, and even now I can't fathom
why I didn't just hold you close—
It would have taken only a moment—
And say whatever it was that I really wanted to say.

III.

I'm watching Batman reruns when the telephone rings.
Holy Charoset, I yell at the kitchen wall, *call back later.*
Maybe I threw some raisins, I don't remember.
We're already married, your mother and I,
but at the time, don't ask, I was living alone.

And so I'm laughing, mostly out of boredom, but still, laughing,
while my father lay dying, gasping for breath in some dirty gutter,
gunned down for a half-empty briefcase, a gefilte fish sandwich,
a *New York Post* which the next day would have his own picture
on the twenty-eighth page; one more dead Jew.

IV.

You burst into the room, fifth grade facts burning your tongue
like Moses' coal. *100 people die every minute,* you tell me, spitting it out,
as I turn down the TV; and then, gleefully: *so since I've been in this room,
and now 75 and now . . . and now . . . and now . . .* O my little census bureau,
my prince of darkness, my prophet of numbers, riddle me this:
how many grains of sand before you can call it a desert?

And where were you the day Kennedy was shot? CNN, interrupting, asks.
My grandmother shakes her head from side to side, clicking her tongue
like she's chopping onions in the old country. *Poor boy,* she says, pointing.
And there's John-John again, still waving that little flag, still saluting.

V.

And who will remember my father when I am gone?
And how many have died since his death?
And what's one more? Or one less?
And what do I know of my father's father?

I'm waiting outside, engine humming, as my son, eighteen, registers.
And now he's shouting, running towards me, arms pumping above his head.
He's Moses the moment before spying the golden calf.
He's his great grandfather crawling underground to freedom.
He's my father flying medical supplies, surviving the crash.
My mother must have held him close. *You're home,* she cries, *safe.*

VI.

Vietnam, I say, or Sarajevo. Afghanistan, my son answers, or Iraq.
My father would have said Germany. He could have said Japan.
Nobody says anonymously. Nobody says Gotham.
Korea, my cousin says, or Kosovo. Maybe he says Iran.
My great grandfather says South Africa. His great grandfather says Spain.
Somebody says Egypt now; somebody, Egypt then.
Nobody says suddenly. Nobody says Brooklyn.

I'm counting myself to sleep, when my wife hears a sound at the door.
Careful, she whispers. We're alone in an empty house, my every breath
reminding me I'm now older than my father on the day of his death.

VII.

There are more people breathing at this very moment, my son insists,
than ever have died. He's home from college, so I don't double-check.
He's driven a long way to surprise me on my birthday. Are you sure
you can't stay, I ask, holding him close. He looks happy, healthy, full of hope;
a woman I've never seen before at his side.

Welcome home, I tell my wife. She's just turned twenty-four.
I'm childless. I'm fatherless. It's the day of the funeral;
Nineteen years still, until the twin towers. Over three thousand since Moses
smashed the commandments. But right now that's not what I'm thinking.
Slowly, she says, guiding me inside of her. How can I not fall back in love?

.

Head of a Man
beneath a Woman's Breast

The Life of Edvard Munch

Author's note:

Edvard Munch (1863–1944), Norwegian painter and printmaker, is best known for his emotionally symbolic paintings, such as *The Scream*. His obsessive images of anxiety and death had a great effect on twentieth-century painting.

Munch's close-knit family life was marked by illness, tragedy, alcoholism, and madness, yet his ability to translate his fear and pain into an artistic vision, eventually led to international acclaim.

A sickly child, Munch barely survived his own birth. His beloved mother Laura Bjolstad, died of consumption when he was five and his sister Sophie died of the same disease at fifteen. (Edvard was fourteen.) His "religiously fanatical" father suffered regular bouts of insanity, as did his younger sister Laura. His brother Andreas died of pneumonia at age thirty. Only Inger, Munch's youngest sister, survived him.

Having confidence in our Lord
who has promised to hear my prayers
I beg for your souls and now
my angels, my lovely dears,
I leave you this letter to let you
know why your mother must leave you.
Your father will guide you to heaven
and I will wait for you there.

—Laura Bjolstad Munch,
on her deathbed, 1868

The Inheritance

I. "Dr. Munch at home with his wife and five children"

Without disease and madness, my life would
be a boat without a rudder.
—E. M.

From my mother the germ of consumption.
From my father the seeds of insanity.
Our King in the kitchen is stirring.

Dear Lord, let this doctor keep walking.
Let his ghosts and his devils distract him.
Let the moment of love never happen.

Near fifty, he's nervous and brooding.
She's twenty-seven, unmarried.
Let him not calm her fever this evening.

Stop the six years of sorrow that follow,
each of the five of us suckling
what we can of her strength for ourselves.

And all we achieve in our lifetimes,
the poems and the music and paintings
won't save her nor render us blameless.

Dear Lord, look how gently he holds her,
as though, in their love there is hope.
For once, I forgive them our future.

II. "The Sick Child (Portrait of Sophie)"

In the same chair that I painted
The Sick Child, all my loved ones,
from my mother on, have been sitting,
waiting for death.

—E. M.

My kittens, *Disease* and *Madness,* scratch
at the bones of my chair, its cane back
a hone for their claws.

Poor angels, Andreas will feed you.
Let Laura comb fleas from your hair.
Inger, the youngest, still fears you,

be gentlest with her when you play.
But stay nearest to Edvard, who named you
(while still in his cradle, they say).

—Sophie Munch, 1877, age 15

Death and the Madonna

*A woman who surrenders herself, finds the pain
filled beauty of the Madonna.*
—E. M.

He approached from behind, like a thief
or a dog; paused trembling near the gold-leaf
framed portrait. Dear Mary, was he drunk,
this youngster, looking more the monk
than the revolutionary;
or, could I be his first . . . he
who espouses free love. Free. Hah! Rich or poor
I say you get what you pay for.
Isn't that the Christian way?
It's those others that lead him astray:
Godless Jaeger, *Christian* Krohg and Heyerdahl—
anarchists all. He, young, listens, his face pale
as death, or worse, these Norwegian winters.
Each brushstroke seems to bleed him of more color
till I can see neither violet, blue, or yellow
but only melancholy and decay, the sorrow
at the moment of fulfillment. There can be
no more paintings of young girls reading,
interiors, or women knitting. And I, I confess,
let my red hair fall, unbutton my white dress
as if I could ease his pain, this Hell
by making myself more beautiful.

                    —Ducha, Berlin, 1890

The Scream

I saw clouds, red as blood and stood
trembling with fear.

—E. M. *(to his sister Laura before her*
admittance to Oslo Hospital for the Insane)

Dear Edvard,
The way men swill raw eggs is why
I still believe in God. The sky
in Oslo drips like ketchup smeared
over the yolk. I never feared
bodily pain, my menstrual flow,
or childbirth. A Jew Andreas knows
(and they're all the same, I'm told)
swears that he'll spit on pork until
we can slaughter pigs and spill
less than a single drop of blood.

Perfection, he won't find here.
Free women, yes; overpriced beer
and all Kristiania's bohemes.
I know what's not or is obscene
and who thinks so; why Kierkegaard's
too full of dread to cross the road
(He's dizzy from too much freedom,
he says. I say it's alcohol
and Nordstrand's blood red evening sun
that sets on all our souls.).

On Ljabroveien when it rains till dusk
and then a winter frost moves in, the gusts
of westward wind will wag the clouds
like tongues of fire. And clear and loud
as if next door, (although it's Ekebergstrand
where the insane asylum stands
between the slaughterhouses and
the house of God) we hear
the screams drown out the prayers.

I pray for us, Edvard, and I cover my ears.

Your loving sister,
Laura, January 1892

Head of a Man beneath a Woman's Breast

Among the millions of stars there are only a few
completely absorbed in each other's flames.

—E. M. *(from a letter to his fiancée Tulla Larsen), 1896*

Love, he says, meaning *manipulation.*
His eyes narrow, close. He sucks like a newborn,
like my one nipple is salt, the other ice;
a cure for consumption. Okay, I say, suck
if it will stop the bleeding. And it does
for a time. But only his.

So when the newspaper prints: *Only Munch*
understands his own paintings,
I cut out: *his own pain*
and send word that I too am dying.

He says: *More than lovers, we're the link*
between generations. He begs: *Never leave me,*
and draws two bodies
absorbed in each other's flames. Still it seems
my dream of the altar's to blame,

but the gun I point at myself
when he cries *deceit* and turns to leave
is not the burden of married life.

Persecution, he says, but to me it means *love,*
closer to truth than his greatest art.
What can I give of more value
than my naked heart.

—Tulla Larsen, 1902
(following her staged suicide attempt,
which ended with Munch shot while
trying to restrain her).

Salome

I should like to bathe my sick soul in your music.
—E. M. *(from a letter to violinist Eva Mudocci), 1903*

It is not true I drew the bow across his throat.
For sympathy he set his head upon my shoulder
where now my Stradivarius rests. His single note
of pain grew to a symphony of anger; at his mother,

Tulla, every saint or whore who had deceived him.
Like the old Florentine painters he did not know
that a woman's proper place is not in Heaven.
If so, then where but Hell is there for us to go

when we need a man's love or another woman's,
or time to play alone and practice our art.
It is not true he drew the lithograph of us
upon the same stone that had fallen from his heart.

The scarf wrapped 'round his neck was for protection.
When he left here that day, he left here whole.
DaVinci would dissect a corpse to see the body's secret music;
For us, he left the slicing of the soul.

—Eva Mudocci, 1904
(a letter to her lover, the pianist
Bella Edwards)

The Nurse: Dr. Jacobsen's Clinic for Nervous Disorders and Alcoholism

My mind is a glass of cloudy water I
must let stand to become clear again.
—E. M., 1908

I. *Madonna,* Munch calls me. *Mother. My Queen.*
But it's *Vampire* when I leave, or *Whore,* or worse.
Tomorrow I turn nineteen. It's my second month as assistant nurse.

II. *Health,* I say, slowly, so that it's *hell* he still expects;
I tell him *drinks without alcohol,* and *cigars with no nicotine,*
but all Munch hears, I think, is *women without sex.*

III. When the camera arrives, Munch, once more, must be obeyed.
As I've molded him, he poses me. My arms folded behind my back
force my breasts forward. I'm unprotected, emboldened, betrayed.

IV. *Notice,* Dr. Jacobsen says, *how all light begins in darkness,*
how what we call the "negative," the photograph's soul,
must be developed slowly, with chemicals and self-control.

V. In the portrait of Dr. Jacobsen, he's part Pope, part libertine:
dressed in clean, pressed whites and venerated by his nurses.
Only afterward will Edvard add Hell's fiery back-screen.

VI. . . . but the image that burns into the plate of my memory
when I enter his sickroom, now studio, to say goodbye
is my own engraved profile, delicate and shy,
the fine threads of my hair gathered like ribbons behind me.

—Sigrid Schacke Andersen,
assistant nurse, 1909

Self Portrait

*Lives there a man in Norway who has not written
the novel of his life?*

—E. M. *(from letters to his sister Inger)*

I. Self Portrait with Burning Cigarette, 1895

To avoid both resemblance and disguise.
How difficult not to look like myself.
To paint, rather, what mother
on her deathbed must have seen
beneath the red of my five-year-old eyes.

II. Self Portrait with Skeleton Arm — 1895

How, on canvas, to distinguish,
the scream from the yawn?

Is her face in the photograph
bored, or calm,
or attentive, as father
recites the third Psalm
and calls us together?

By dawn, she was gone.

I remember how tightly
Death's jaws were drawn,
as if embarrassed by her smell
and the thinness of her arms.

III. Self Portrait in Hell, 1895

My face, burnt from the sun,
glowed like a searchlight set
upon the paleness of my body
when I removed my clothes
to join Andreas in the ocean.
I brought along my camera
but Andre appears in shadow
while I'm crowned by sunlight's halo.
I had to turn my eyes,
so brightly did the heavens
reflect off of the water
like flames rising from below.

IV. Self Portrait with Brushes, 1904

Like a thief on the gallows whom no one mourns,
my exhibit hangs to public scorn.
Only the insane could paint like this—
and desire publicity's Judas kiss.

V. Self Portrait in Distress, 1919

I am badly dressed
and my portraits please
only the sitter's enemies,
who praise the likeness.
The subject will not pay!

As for the German press
they see only excess,
melancholy, and decay.

Has man ever more plainly
stated what he means?
The French paint what they see,
I, what I have seen.

VI. Self Portrait with Stick of Pastel (age 80), 1943

He was a boy, this Nazi sent to warn me
to evacuate in fourteen days or suffer
the consequences of the German army.
It's madness, Pops, to live alone at your age.

As if I'm not surrounded by my children;
sixty years of drawings. Every painting
ever lost or sold, I have repainted.
The closets are unused except for storage.

Not madness, son, but alcohol's what nearly killed me,
and damned affairs with women I could not rely on.
I risked my hands with every brawl or blackout.
But here I'm harmless; kids call me *the hermit,*

and finally I've found peace. So let the fascists
fight their hellish war. I am not leaving.
They call my work *degenerate* in Munich
where soldiers storm museums and shoot my paintings.

But my one oil with ten holes will outlast
ten of their works whole. I leave to Oslo,
my childhood home, all my possessions.
Death is to my art as a mother to her children.

Edvard Munch died one month after his eightieth birthday. All of his works were left to the city of Oslo. These included more than one thousand oils, four thousand watercolors and drawings, and sixteen thousand impressions of his graphics.

The March
of the Orphans

The March of the Orphans
August 5, 1942

*All residents of the Korczak Children's Home
will report to the Gdansk Rail Station for
resettlement.*

—*Posted notice*

*I assert with joy that with few exceptions,
man is a creature of goodness and understanding.*

—*Janusz Korczak*, How to Love a Child

How simply my children, like newborn pups,
jostle each other, barking for stories,
words tossed their way like coins
to a blind man who rattles his cup
more for sound than for money.

I tell them of young Dmitry Tolstoy, sighing
over his mother's grave; his brother Leo
scribbling notes. Suddenly the guests arrive.
Dmitry straightens himself, wipes his eyes.
Leo pounds the earth and weeps.

The lessons I teach, I teach myself.
These children desire to change
their world. If I cry for them now,
it's to keep the world from changing me.
Read, they beg, chapters from your life's work,

how the famed Dr. Korczak, physician and poet,
self-proclaimed father of all orphans,
took us in and gave us hope.
But my voice sounds strange to me,
weak, even foolish. Reminiscence

makes the saddest literature,
my Stefa scolds. How old she looks
among the scrubbed, expectant children.
It's harder to live one day with honor,
she tells them, than to write a book

as great as any the world has known.
She calls me mad. I've no response
except more words. This morning,
Stefa by my side, I'll lead
along Krochmalna Street two hundred

of our sons and daughters. Proudly
clad in Sabbath clothes, we'll line up
four abreast and sing so loudly all Warsaw
will hear our joyous song. I'll kiss Stefa
and if there's time, recite some poems

before, like wild dogs, we're slaughtered.

Interrogation

Pregnant women were ordered to stand an hour on one leg. If their foot touched ground, they were told, their stomachs would be pierced.
—H. O. Treblinka, 1943

We lift our legs.
Dogs peeing. O Pavlova: In the mausoleum
that is my womb, my child crouches
like the dying swan, while I spin
on point, pirouette until, like Elijah,
I begin to rise.

Dirt breeds lice,
lice typhus. How improbably long
our bodies remain alive. Today, twice
I have escaped selection. My legs, grown strong,
balance against death like a dancer
frozen between question and answer,
performance and applause.

My art
is inseparable from my grief. The earth,
like a davening Jew, starts to sway. My heart
teeters, doubles its beat. Each breath
in Hell is an act of resistance.
I tell my heavy feet to dance.

Faraway Landscape

pen and ink uncovered in Buchenwald, 1944

An artist in our midst. Fool,
I tell myself, why risk
what little life I've left
to steal him ink and pen.
He gives no thanks. He thinks
it natural. I have my task
as he has his.
O, how I've come to hate
his scratching late each night,
his fruit trees carved
into some moldy crust of bread.
He doesn't care that starved
men envy their own dead.
He hears our cries but will not
document our pain. Instead . . .
he draws, knowing each line
could be his last, some Palestine,
some faraway landscape
as if he could escape this world
imagining the future
or the past.

Christmas Eve
Theresienstadt, 1944

*Burosova escaped death by impressing a Nazi
officer who had ordered her to paint a picture
of the Madonna.*

This tear you've drawn, in Mary's eye:
so real, I'm moved to kiss it dry

and so, I offer you this gift:
your life. You are a clever Jew,

a jewel, and I pledge to you
as long as I'm oberführer

you'll have occasion for your art.
Design for me a Christmas scene

more beautiful than nature's own.
Its quiet peace could help to ease

your people's pain. Instead you choose
to document their suffering.

What cultured woman does not know
a child's death cannot be drawn

in reds and greens. I'll say it plain:
your horror pales next to our own

that's drawn from flesh. I don't expect
for my kindness, your gratitude,

but learn to turn the other cheek.
You draw and draw. Why won't you speak?

Young Men Painting
Warsaw Ghetto, 1943

(Gela Seksztein 1907–1943)

I want my wife to be remembered!
My Gela was an *artist*. True,
she wasn't honored in this lifetime,
but she explained the latest theories

at our ghetto school. Renoir, the Frenchman,
with his robust women dancing out of doors
has been remembered. That breasts and thighs,
these days, still cause smooth cheeks to redden

is no small miracle. Can these youths be the same
who've seen their sisters shamed, then spat upon
or beaten? What Muse could whisper *Beautiful,*
and tempt them to remember what a young man

would of women. Desire stings their souls
the way Degas, to stir the flesh would chill
the day's bathwater. My daughter Margolit
deserves, at forty months, to be remembered also.

She mastered Yiddish perfectly and each night hid
her lesson books beneath the stairway.
Years from this day, among my wife's dark images
of young men painting, you will find them.

Bathing by Candlelight

Nude Women Bathing, Drying Themselves, and Combing Their Hair

I show them as animals, cleaning themselves.
—*Edgar Degas*

Old men should marry, Monsieur Degas. Time moves
too slowly to live alone. There are days to bathe,
to wash, to dry yourself. It's late in life
one learns to read. Early, we aim to finish the book
or write our own. Is it indifference or fear
that calls tame what is caged or clean? Put down your brush
and don't despair if your purring wife, breasts bared,
when you turn from your canvas says:
That's a pretty thing you've drawn,
and turns her back to comb her hair.

We comb our hair and dry our backs, but should we pause
to scratch too thick or skinny thighs,
with patient and attentive hate
of all that's unrefined and coarse, you wait
but will not look away. Later you'll sketch
a body twisted out of shape, crouched
like a frog's. But why do you obscure the face?
We let you watch us wash ourselves
because you call us beautiful
and paint us common, without grace.

At the Moulin Rouge

. . . physically, an ugly dwarf who led a dissolute life . . .
—The History of Art, *H. W. Janson*

Painting? It will not give me back my legs.
—*Henri de Toulouse-Lautrec*

One bass string snaps, silently licks the air
and curls like the tongue of a chorus girl
along her lower lip. He sees this and draws
stockings tossed casually over a stool,
the moment before they slip down,
sleeping dogs at my feet.
Stay, he begs,
sketching my left leg
with a single black line to support its weight;
my right thigh is kicked high, heavy and muscular
as a prize filly's.
Here, at the Rouge, we girls are everything
he dreams about, the light
discovering our legs each night
with the only language he will ever understand.
Tonight, if by chance, I danced into his heart,
would he speak to me of love,
or the limitations of art?

Study for Nude Bathing by Candlelight

The mystery of simplicity is the most
unfathomable of all mysteries.
—*Pierre Bonnard*

No effect of light, no theorem shows
how a woman can become a streak
of mauve; her face, a faded rose.
Nabi he's named himself; he speaks

religiously. The bourgeoisie
demand of art the right to dream.
They've time for that. My luxury's
this tub. I keep my body clean

then wash his clothes. Nighttime, I pose
(unposed for authenticity)
nude in the bath. I've read his prose:
credos on art's great mystery

but sketches of my breasts expose
no more than sentimentality
and the candle's glow. I do not know
why, in my domesticity,

men see such things: sensuality,
a mother's love. Of cooks they dream,
and parlor maids to serve them tea
in tiny cups. I pour the cream.

Pierre stirs, sips. Next he'll propose
that I unbutton my chemise.
He slips his glasses from his nose.
Nearsighted, he'll paint what he sees.

Woman with Mango

You call me madman, savage; she calls me God.
—Paul Gauguin, from a letter to his wife

Paris! Dance halls! Why chant ancient prayers;
worship gods who cannot summon angels to appear?
True, he has children, a wife. Who could compare
my dark life to theirs? *Black,* he commands, and I hear
lightning crack, the wind that carries all women's tears
to their faithless lovers. But then he draws me near
and my color vibrates, like music, sweetening the air
we sleep under. His heart, dull drum that summons his cares,
holds its beat. He dreams, perhaps, of his career,
Le Louvre, stocks, fame. How can I calm fears
I don't understand? I sing, stroke his hair,
bring maiore and mango. How queer
life must be in Paris. What will the ladies wear,
I wonder, in the cabarets this year?

Portrait of Hortense Fiquet

Does an apple move?
—Paul Cézanne

Does an apple move? Five hours a day,
day after day, I sit. *Still life with Fiquet*
I call it. This is no portrait. The papered wall
contains more passion than my face.
When my muscles cramp, he rages,
waves his thick housepainter's hands.
Does an apple move!

     The Ball, Zola calls me,
as if I were a weight at Paul's ankle.
Who's chained to whom? Move? I'm unmarried,
young Paul already seven. I am a mistress
and a servant. Who else would sit so still.
Months pass, flowers wither
waiting for his finishing touch.

     A genius?
Or mad. He has no horse sense. *Hortense,*
he crows, *a kilo of green is greener*
than half a kilo. He knows I dream
of Switzerland, snow, laced like wedding gowns;
And Paris, floor shows and dance halls. *Fifty francs,*
I answer, *is greater than twenty-five.*

     Paul's father, bourgeois,
forever alive, has halved our allowance:
A sum suitable for a single man.
He's seen his son's child by a seamstress
and doesn't approve. Paul, near forty, balding, nods.
Terrified, he paints, while we starve, fresh fruit
rotting on our table. It decays, turns bitter inside,
        but does not move.

Reclining Woman with Skirt Upturned

They damn their parent's love, who deny sex.
—E. S.

On April 13, 1912, at age 22, Egon Schiele was
imprisoned on charges of corrupting a minor—his
companion and model, Walli Neuzil. His brushes
and pens were confiscated but he continued to draw
on the prison walls, using his own "bitter spit."

. . . and we watched
as my flesh dried and faded, disappearing
into the bare gray walls: my private parts,
he said, for private viewing. And when his thirst
grew unbearable, we'd kiss good-bye,
my moist tongue slipping his a gift
greater than any food or file.

Has Egon murdered,
raped, set fires? There is no child,
ignorant of passion. And yet the judge,
who counts himself among the educated class,
in court, over a candle, burned—
to save his son from sex and modern art—
myself reclining with my skirt upturned.

Reclining Nude 1917

If a woman poses for you, she must give herself
to you.
—*Modigliani*

I give to you my body still blushing ochre, rose and peach
while my face remains proud and eager for admiration

You give to me your hand, delicately boned with its thin beautiful fingers
and your eyes with the gentleness of a horse that has been beaten

I give to you my spirit, its naked arrogance and the almonds of my eyes,
which you, knowing the futility of capturing the soul's mystery, close

I give to you the angled nose and sculptured head of the ancient queens
of Egypt. You give to me the subdued fire of the prophets of Israel

You give to me the handsomest man in Paris whose paintings will not sell
and when, in time, you mistake the impassioned cry of a wounded animal

for the hot pigment of eroticism, I will take your life and you
will be remembered, if at all, for the way you gave yourself to me

Rouge

Perfection is possible.
—Picasso

Because neither the carved scroll of the violin
nor its first slow moan of music
can explain the dance of the bow
like Demosthene's tongue

     and because Baudelaire
could recite his poems long after he ceased
to recognize his own eyes in the mirror

     I let your thumbs slide
down the thin black seams of my stockings.

Because my mother, her neck slender and delicate
as Modigliani's reason, sketched her dreams
on the pale powdered canvas
of her face

     and because you, too, are a beautician,
your talent covering nature's outrageous birthmarks
with the abstract unity of beauty;

Because false words leave their mark,
like the faint smudge of rouge
on a lover's lips

     and because the memory of our love
will shine in your mind
with a sequin's brilliant but momentary spark

     I leave you with the silence
of a woman undressing in the dark.

Marie Nursing Her Daughter

*My greatest mistake was choosing painting
rather than motherhood.*

—*Mary Cassatt, 1905*

It is the beauty of your face
which has nothing to do with men
painting for men, with Degas or Manet.
Renoir's teenaged niece, already serving tea,
lets her shy breasts poke through a pink chemise.
"I do not admit," Degas crows, "that a woman can draw
like a man." Dear Sir, I agree.

I need no nakedness to distract the viewer.
I remember the moment my mother's heart stopped,
but before her brain could know, the news
spread halfway up her spine; her hands
in mine. "A woman's happiness,"
she used to say, "is to bear children.
For whose sake did nature make you a woman?"

And always I wrote to her of printmaking.
"Paris," she'd answer "is no place for ladies."
"Imagine if Degas pursued his career
 between baking and nursing," I dared not write back.
At such odd angles we'd correspond for thirty years. I'm sixty-one
and now, I ask myself: For whose sake?
There is no lack of women painters.

But paintings of women! Apart from their relation
to men. The moment the nursing child first knows
she is no longer a part of her mother;
what man could see that?
When you speak to me about your daughter
there is a beauty in your face.
I will capture the feminine or I will have failed.

The Jews
that We Are

The Jews that We Are

. . . you have inherited its burden without its mystery.
—Elie Wiesel

I. March 1979 and I am watching Nazis
march through Chicago. The bold type
of the *Sun-Times* describes a small band
of hoodlums, undereducated boy scouts, the better
to be ignored. My grandfather, back hunched
over his Bible, agrees. Jews like myself
should stay home, should lay down our stones
and pray like the Jews that we are.

II. Grandfather, you are easy to love
with your long beard and the way you sway
like a palm branch in the storm. It is easy
to romanticize your spiritual search,
worldly naiveté and wise rabbinical words.
You belong in the books I read
by Singer, Peretz, Shalom Aleichem.
But their characters are ignorant
of the chapters to come. You know
where their prayers will lead.

III. A circle. Six Nazis. Your wife in the middle.
One soldier says all *Jewesses* are whores
and the others agree. You say nothing.
Years later you'll decide to speak:
"Do we not serve Hitler's purpose, we
who would sooner renounce our beliefs
than assume our burdens?"

IV. A generation after the Holocaust
and I know no Hebrew. No Yiddish. No Torah.
I fast only on the Day of Atonement
and even then I've been known to cheat.
A generation after the Holocaust
and I apologize for my grandfather's
bent back and wild gestures.
I used to tremble to the rhythm
of his prayers. I feared the mysterious
words that kept us from the devil.
Now, from my window I watch Nazis march.
Their feet strike the pavement
like the ticking of a clock. I am a Jew
a generation after the Holocaust.
Poorer, my grandfather says, without a past
than he, who has no future.

The Queen Esther Award

*. . . The criteria considered by the celebrity judges are
spirituality, beauty and commitment to a life of service.*

—Jewish Weekly News

*How can I endure to see the evil that shall come upon
my kindred?*

—*Book of* Esther

*In the most inconceivable places,
Auschwitz for one, competitions were held
for the cleanest barracks. I can't stand clutter
to this day,* my grandmother whispers,
although you'd think I would feel the opposite way.

I shift in my seat. On stage
the evil Haman clowns and rages, confides
his plan of genocide, his hate
for Mordecai the Jew. The children boo
and shake their fists. Grandmother hisses
and stomps her feet. No one's afraid.
Behind me—the smell of Purim cookies,
for the party that follows this masquerade.

My daughter is Queen Esther for an hour.
I pray that each line we practiced stays with her.
At eight, she barely remembers her speeches
but knows she was chosen for her beauty
which, pleasing the King,
will save her people.

*We lined up and they looked us over.
Celebrity judges? Mengele, Hoess.
"Filth," they said. "Dogs!" My head was shaved.
If there were mirrors I'd have taken my life
and the lives of my children.*

My daughter runs towards me but girlfriends
engulf her. Laughing, they lift the crown
from her head. Each tries it on and poses
for the others. I marvel at the beauty
of these young Jewish girls
with their long braided hair,
looking nothing like the children
of the children
of survivors.

What to Tell Your Children about Nuclear War
Lecture Hall B, 8 P.M., Monday 24th

After her bath, she's still naked,
down on her knees, scrubbing the tub.
Nesting, Spock calls it.
the insatiable urge to sanitize.
I'm sweating through my suit, daydreaming
about surprising her from behind. Never
have I wanted, so badly, to hold her,
to populate this filthy world
I swore I would not bring children into.

Already I'm late. I've missed the cruise missile
and the silo debate, but I hand my wife her robe
and let her rest my head in what we're calling
the cradle of civilization. "Listen,"
she whispers, and I do hear something,
deep underground; a heartbeat,
like the tiniest test explosions.

"Tell us," my wife says, "a story." She's read
that even before birth, infants recognize
their father's voice, find it reassuring.
I'm curled in her lap, feeling safe
and thinking about the Rabbis of the Talmud
and the laws of the Jewish High Court;
How no man could serve as judge
before the raising of children
humbled, and made him wise.

Where I Sat
What I Ate

I sat between
Bubbeh
and Aunt Bet
I never had a prayer

Bubbeh fingered
her forearm
the five numbers
burnt there
and

that's how I learned
to count
Aunt Bet

told lies about boys
who had loved her
when she was
a young coquette
I sat

like the silence
between train whistles
and dreamt

of the first woman
who taught me to dance
She was so beautiful
I never had a chance

Her skin was
as smooth as
her silence
I sat

like a boy mid-bath
between curiosity and
my own nakedness
I sat

between Bubbeh
and Aunt Bet
Between
spoonfuls of regret
I ate

from this you shouldn't know
and
may you never forget

For Forty Years My Mother

For forty years my mother clipped the wings
of newspapers, stories of men's memories,

unable to fly, rising suddenly, like smoke.
Today, in Israel, as Yom Ha'Shoah approaches

computers are programmed to find family
and friends. "Remember?" my mother asks,

as her sisters flood Jerusalem, City of Belief.
They input dates, towns, names. "Wait,"

they beg their children, "just a bit longer."
But already we're drowning in a Red Sea of grief,

longing for the dryness of the desert.

Recital

Blessed is the Lord who trains my hands for battle,
my fingers for warfare.
—*Psalm 144*

I. The Original Poem

My hands, French-braiding my daughter's hair before her recital,
are suddenly my grandmother's, kneading the ceremonial Friday night challah—
the same dark veins, the Tigris, the Euphrates, spreading life into each tributary.

Or turned palms up, eight trains arriving at the same station, at the same time,
two others already emptied and heading back out, boxcars with pet names
like the racing boats of the wealthy: *Interior Affairs, Foreign Policy.*

Or elbows held close to the body, ten escape routes, and two shtetls
—my great grandmother in one, my great grandfather in the other.
I'm holding them both in my hands; I'm like God in the old camp song,
when my daughter starts to play, and I, forgetting myself, clap
and keep clapping, and I think maybe this world is like God's boat
and He calls it *Genocide,* and the next world is also His and ours to share.

II. Foreign Policy

Recital is the name of the poem I was reading at my first recital;
my voice strung tight as young David's slingshot, his first war stretched
between his sinewy hands. This is the battle he would sing about, years later.
But first he had to learn to play the lyre, practice poetry and song,
love and prayer. So much work just to celebrate his victory.

Imagine him at the slaughterhouse, choosing the sheep, cutting its guts,
his grandmother working quickly beside him, keeping the casing fresh
to insure the sensuous quality of the sound. She separates the fat,
rinses off the excrement, removing the membranes, except for the muscle fiber,
while David, his thick thumbs bleeding now,
dries, and braids the hanks. Music fit for a King.

III. Genocide

Recital is the name of the poem I was reading at my first recital,
when, in the back, I heard somebody's grandmother shuffling down the
    hallway,
her whole bridge game, Slavic barges, in tow, and suddenly
chairs were scraping all over the place. *Speak up,* she says, *what are you saying?*
I'm reading the numbers on her forearm, each numeral a poem written by
    God:
perfect, meaningless, and containing all meaning, just as you'd expect in a
    poem
by the Poet Laureate of all universes, of all religions, of all time.

IV. Interior Affairs

My wife's already in the kitchen baking cookies for our daughter's first recital
when I sit down for breakfast. Somewhere it's nighttime: bombs are falling
and children are starving; but I'm pouring the milk and the sugar,
whistling a song and nibbling the nape of my lover's neck
on my way back to the refrigerator; and neither of us can guess
who will eventually find the cunning enemy, cancer,
hiding like a secret code ring in the cereal box of the body.

V. Battles

All this, I'm remembering, was years ago, but years later I'm re-reading
   Recital
to my daughter who turned out to be a pianist after all
and is practicing for her own recital, at the same North Shore Jewish
   Nursing Home,
her grandmother mired in the mud of the waiting list and the whole family
   conspiring
to maneuver her to the front of the line. She's the last soldier standing be-
   tween me
and my death. She's the pre-Columbus boat heading over the edge of the
   horizon,
and I'm the nameless little boat following. Her husband died in the war of
   the streets
and her brother died in the war to end all wars and her father died in the war
   before that.
And the personal war my wife and I have waged between us for so long
that it's beginning to look like nostalgia, only seems never-ending. I want to
   die,
not like Saul, on the battlefield of my own sword, nor like Solomon, my
   house in disarray,
but like David, in his bed, reciting the psalms, at war only with his own soul.

VI. Lullabies

I'm standing in the back of the room listening to my daughter's recital,
her fingers furiously pumping up and down, and now, diminuendo toward
    the end,
controlling the strings and valves of my heart. Maybe I am the sheep,
sacrificing my inner life for the sake of her song. Or maybe her palms and
    fingers,
resting face down on the keys, are only her palms and fingers resting.

I'm alone in the back of the room, a sentry guarding the free cookies
which, according to policy, cannot be eaten except in the recreation hall
we call *The Afterlife*. Otherwise, no one would sit still for the music,
half the audience deaf, and the rest already sailing home on the faint breath
of the small boats they've christened *Battles* and *Lullabies*. I want to die,
not like Goliath, a victim of modern warfare, nor like Uriah, turned love's
    collateral damage,
but like David himself, a shepherd leading his flock to feed among the
    flowers.

VII. The Revision

Would you still love me, my daughter asks, if I had played all the wrong
    notes?
She's wondering what it means to be her: Jewish, American, and upper-
    middle class
in a time of war, when all she really wants to think about is poetry and song.

Would you still love me, my wife asks, if I were old, ugly, too thin, toothless?
She's bombing her own body weekly, shrapnel embedded
in the roof and walls of the holy house where we prayed and made love.

Would you still love me, David asked his God, if I killed a man
for no better reason than to take his beautiful wife as my lover?

Would you still love me, I asked my father, if instead of fighting my own
    battles,
I deserted, conscientiously objected, sat on the sidelines, writing,
without even once harnessing the power to revise my life like words on a
    page?

Would you still love me, God asked my grandmother in the reception hall
before His grand recital, if I wiped out your entire family, let's say all at once,
leaving only one self-involved American tributary to tell the tale?

Life, my grandmother once explained to me, is not poetry, never was, and
    was
never meant to be. Now by way of answer I watch her wipe away the faint
    smudge
of chocolate still fresh on God's lips. *Your grandmother's one tough cookie,*
He whispers to me, while she rustles about, her chair scraping every which
    way.
What? she asks. *Speak up, or no one will hear a word you are saying.*
As for your certain and coming death, she adds,
I don't know if you're a religious man, but you might try praying.

> *Your steadfast love is eternal. Do not forsake the work*
> *of your hands.*
> —Psalm 138

Acknowledgments

ANTHOLOGIES

Norton Introduction to Poetry (Norton, 1998), "Undressing Aunt Frieda"
Beyond Lament: Poets of the World Bearing Witness to the Holocaust
   (Northwestern University Press, 1998), "March of the Orphans"
Unsettling America: Contemporary Multicultural Poetry (Viking, 1994,)
   "Undressing Aunt Frieda"
Men of Our Time: Male Poetry in Contemporary America (University of
   Georgia Press 1992), "Undressing Aunt Frieda"
Blood to Remember: American Poets on the Holocaust (Texas Tech University
   Press 1991), "The Jews That We Are," "Undressing Aunt Frieda"
Without a Single Answer: Poems on Contemporary Israel (Judah Magnes
   Museum, 1990) "For Forty Years My Mother"
Ghosts of the Holocaust (Wayne State University Press, 1989), "Faraway
   Landscape," "The Jews That We Are," "Interrogation," "The Queen Esther
   Award," "Where I Sat"

AWARDS

New Letters Literary Award: "Salome," "Head of a Man Beneath A Woman's
   Breast"
Felix Pollack Prize in Poetry, *Madison Review*: "Undressing My Daughter,"
   "Undressing Aunt Frieda," "I Wish He Had Died Then, His Body"
Billee Murray Denny Award: "Woman With Mango"
Pablo Neruda Prize (Finalist), *Nimrod Magazine*: "Young Men Painting,"
   "Interrogation," "The March of the Orphans"
SCAA International Poetry Competition: "Nude Woman Bathing, Drying
   Themselves and Washing their Hair"

MAGAZINES

Poetry Northwest: "Death and the Madonna," "Portrait of Hortense Fiquet,"
   "Reclining Woman with Upturned Skirt"
New England Watershed: "What to Tell Your Children about Nuclear War"

New Letters, "The Scream," "Head of a Man Beneath a Woman's Breast,"
  "Salome"
Southern Review, "Recital"

BOOK

The poems in Section II, "Head of a Man Beneath a Woman's Breast," were
  previously printed in a limited edition book, *Semblant* (Gehenna Press,
  1996), along with lithographs by Leonard Baskin.

Richard Michelson was born in Brooklyn, New York. His previous publications include *Tap Dancing for Relatives* and two fine press collaborations with the artist Leonard Baskin, *Masks* and *Semblant*. Among the major anthologies that include his poems are *The Norton Introduction to Poetry* and *Unsettling America: Contemporary American Multicultural Poetry*. Michelson is also the author of numerous award-winning children's books, including *Happy Feet, Ten Times Better,* and the highly lauded *Too Young for Yiddish*. Michelson is the owner of R. Michelson Galleries in Northampton, Massachusetts. His Web site is www.RMichelson.com.

ILLINOIS POETRY SERIES
Laurence Lieberman, Editor

History Is Your Own Heartbeat
Michael S. Harper (1971)

The Foreclosure
Richard Emil Braun (1972)

The Scrawny Sonnets and Other
Narratives
Robert Bagg (1973)

The Creation Frame
Phyllis Thompson (1973)

To All Appearances: Poems New and
Selected
Josephine Miles (1974)

The Black Hawk Songs
Michael Borich (1975)

Nightmare Begins Responsibility
Michael S. Harper (1975)

The Wichita Poems
Michael Van Walleghen (1975)

Images of Kin: New and Selected
Poems
Michael S. Harper (1977)

Poems of the Two Worlds
Frederick Morgan (1977)

Cumberland Station
Dave Smith (1977)

Tracking
Virginia R. Terris (1977)

Riversongs
Michael Anania (1978)

On Earth as It Is
Dan Masterson (1978)

Coming to Terms
Josephine Miles (1979)

Death Mother and Other Poems
Frederick Morgan (1979)

Goshawk, Antelope
Dave Smith (1979)

Local Men
James Whitehead (1979)

Searching the Drowned Man
Sydney Lea (1980)

With Akhmatova at the Black Gates
Stephen Berg (1981)

Dream Flights
Dave Smith (1981)

More Trouble with the Obvious
Michael Van Walleghen (1981)

The American Book of the Dead
Jim Barnes (1982)

The Floating Candles
Sydney Lea (1982)

Northbook
Frederick Morgan (1982)

Collected Poems, 1930–83
Josephine Miles (1983; reissue, 1999)

The River Painter
Emily Grosholz (1984)

Healing Song for the Inner Ear
Michael S. Harper (1984)

The Passion of the Right-Angled Man
T. R. Hummer (1984)

Dear John, Dear Coltrane
Michael S. Harper (1985)

Poems from the Sangamon
John Knoepfle (1985)

In It
Stephen Berg (1986)

Songlines in Michaeltree: New and
Collected Poems
Michael S. Harper (2000)

Pursuit of a Wound
Sydney Lea (2000)

The Pebble: Old and New Poems
Mairi MacInnes (2000)

Chance Ransom
Kevin Stein (2000)

House of Poured-Out Waters
Jane Mead (2001)

The Silent Singer: New and Selected
Poems
Len Roberts (2001)

The Salt Hour
J. P. White (2001)

Guide to the Blue Tongue
Virgil Suárez (2002)

The House of Song
David Wagoner (2002)

X =
Stephen Berg (2002)

Arts of a Cold Sun
G. E. Murray (2003)

Barter
Ira Sadoff (2003)

The Hollow Log Lounge
R. T. Smith (2003)

In the Black Window: New and
Selected Poems
Michael Van Walleghen (2004)

A Deed to the Light
Jeanne Murray Walker (2004)

Controlling the Silver
Lorna Goodison (2005)

Good Morning and Good Night
David Wagoner (2005)

American Ghost Roses
Kevin Stein (2005)

Battles and Lullabies
Richard Michelson (2005)

NATIONAL POETRY SERIES

Eroding Witness
Nathaniel Mackey (1985)
Selected by Michael S. Harper

Palladium
Alice Fulton (1986)
Selected by Mark Strand

Cities in Motion
Sylvia Moss (1987)
Selected by Derek Walcott

The Hand of God and a Few
Bright Flowers
William Olsen (1988)
Selected by David Wagoner

The Great Bird of Love
Paul Zimmer (1989)
Selected by William Stafford

Stubborn
Roland Flint (1990)
Selected by Dave Smith

The Surface
Laura Mullen (1991)
Selected by C. K. Williams

The Dig
Lynn Emanuel (1992)
Selected by Gerald Stern

My Alexandria
Mark Doty (1993)
Selected by Philip Levine

The High Road to Taos
Martin Edmunds (1994)
Selected by Donald Hall

Theater of Animals
Samn Stockwell (1995)
Selected by Louise Glück

The Broken World
Marcus Cafagña (1996)
Selected by Yusef Komunyakaa

Nine Skies
A. V. Christie (1997)
Selected by Sandra McPherson

Lost Wax
Heather Ramsdell (1998)
Selected by James Tate

So Often the Pitcher Goes to Water
until It Breaks
Rigoberto González (1999)
Selected by Ai

Renunciation
Corey Marks (2000)
Selected by Philip Levine

Manderley
Rebecca Wolff (2001)
Selected by Robert Pinsky

Theory of Devolution
David Groff (2002)
Selected by Mark Doty

Rhythm and Booze
Julie Kane (2003)
Selected by Maxine Kumin

Shiva's Drum
Stephen Cramer (2004)
Selected by Grace Schulman

The Welcome
David Friedman (2005)
Selected by Stephen Dunn

OTHER POETRY VOLUMES

Local Men and *Domains*
James Whitehead (1987)

Her Soul beneath the Bone: Women's
Poetry on Breast Cancer
Edited by Leatrice Lifshitz (1988)

Days from a Dream Almanac
Dennis Tedlock (1990)

Working Classics: Poems on Industrial
Life
Edited by Peter Oresick and Nicholas Coles
(1990)

Hummers, Knucklers, and Slow
Curves: Contemporary Baseball Poems
Edited by Don Johnson (1991)

The Double Reckoning of Christopher
Columbus
Barbara Helfgott Hyett (1992)

Selected Poems
Jean Garrigue (1992)

New and Selected Poems, 1962–92
Laurence Lieberman (1993)

The Dig and *Hotel Fiesta*
Lynn Emanuel (1994)

For a Living: The Poetry of Work
Edited by Nicholas Coles and Peter Oresick
(1995)

The Tracks We Leave: Poems on
Endangered Wildlife of North America
Barbara Helfgott Hyett (1996)

Peasants Wake for Fellini's *Casanova*
and Other Poems
*Andrea Zanzotto; edited and translated
by John P. Welle and Ruth Feldman;
drawings by Federico Fellini and Augusto
Murer* (1997)

Moon in a Mason Jar and *What My
Father Believed*
Robert Wrigley (1997)

The Wild Card: Selected Poems, Early
and Late
*Karl Shapiro; edited by Stanley Kunitz
and David Ignatow* (1998)

Turtle, Swan and *Bethlehem in Broad
Daylight*
Mark Doty (2000)

Illinois Voices: An Anthology of
Twentieth-Century Poetry
Edited by Kevin Stein and G. E. Murray
(2001)

On a Wing of the Sun
Jim Barnes (3-volume reissue, 2001)

Poems
*William Carlos Williams; introduction by
Virginia M. Wright-Peterson* (2002)

Creole Echoes: The Francophone
Poetry of Nineteenth-Century
Louisiana
*Translated by Norman R. Shapiro;
introduction and notes by M. Lynn Weiss*
(2003)

Poetry from *Sojourner:* A Feminist
Anthology
*Edited by Ruth Lepson with Lynne
Yamaguchi; introduction by Mary
Loeffelholz* (2004)

Asian American Poetry: The Next
Generation
*Edited by Victoria M. Chang; foreword by
Marilyn Chin* (2004)

Papermill: Poems, 1927–35
Joseph Kalar; edited by Ted Genoways
(2005)

The University of Illinois Press
is a founding member of the
Association of American University Presses.

Composed in 10/14 Carter & Cone Galliard
by Celia Shapland
for the University of Illinois Press
Designed by Copenhaver Cumpston
Manufactured by The Maple-Vail Book
Manufacturing Group

University of Illinois Press
1325 South Oak Street
Champaign, IL 61820-6903
www.press.uillinois.edu